HOW TO
DRAW & PAINT
STILL LIFE

HOW TO
DRAW & PAINT
STILL LIFE

A QUINTET BOOK

Published by Chartwell Books Inc.,
A Division of Book Sales Inc.,
110 Enterprise Avenue,
Secaucus, New Jersey 07094

ISBN 1-55521-053-8

This book was designed and produced by
Quintet Publishing Limited
6 Blundell Street, London N7

Editorial Director: Jeremy Harwood
Art Director: Robert Morley
Editors: Victoria Funk, Judy Martin
Art Editor: Neville Graham

Printed in Hong Kong by Leefung-Asco
Printers Limited

HOW TO DRAW & PAINT
STILL LIFE

CONTENTS

Still life

STILL LIFE PAINTING has been the sole preoccupation of several important artists throughout the centuries and virtually the sole interest of a smaller number. On many occasions a school of artists has earned a reputation solely on the high quality of its still life pictures. Still life can be any one of a variety of things from a group of objects related to each other by association, as in a collection of objects used in hunting or cooking, to a series of apparently disparate items placed on a surface or across several surfaces. Often stories are told by still lifes, which appear as foreground or background accompanying a figure or maybe more than one figure. Otherwise, the set-up might well be simply one affording the artist the opportunity to exploit formal niceties, such as colour relationships, textural rendering, or compositions of a particular kind.

Masters of the still life

The brilliant use of still life objects in the early paintings of the 17th century artist Velazquez are as strong in form and structure as they are in the faithful rendering of color and texture. A glazed pot shimmers in the sunlight as the figure holding it almost breathes the air about him. Chardin, an 18th century French artist, painted intimate interiors reflecting daily events of little consequence in themselves, but lovingly depicted. The demands for both a rural element and the picturesque no doubt were factors in persuading these artists to cherish and cultivate such skills.

Notable for the full union of figure with still life painting are several Dutch painters of the 18th century, particularly Jan Vermeer (1632–1675). These pictures have a strong narrative element, almost elusive in their description and suggestion of a specific event; the artist painting a portrait, the girl having a music lesson, and such subjects, all of which demand that the setting, far from being staged as though in the proscenium arch on a stage, is casual and everyday. To render convincing contexts, Vermeer spent time on careful,

Velazquez, 'The Kitchen Scene with Christ'. The skill with which Velazquez

8

was able to render both still life and figures is apparent in this painting. Note how objects are treated with as much care as the figures.

closely observed interiors and the objects within them. He was a master at rendering the texture of crisp cotton or the languid, weighty drop of silk. Pewter or silver take on a verisimilitude to the appearance of the original; convincing and yet unmistakably painted. The good artist would never let illusion or reality detach him from the so-called 'formal values' of enjoying the picture surface.

A fine exponent of the still life was the 19th century artist Paul Cézanne, a great painter and innovator whose system of working required long periods of readjustment and reworking, overpainting and corrections. The still life group was thus an obvious subject, allowing him to carry on his trials and experiments without the problems of movement. Color was used to organize and unify the design, and the space was carefully composed so that the eye travelled across, through, beyond, around and below the picture surface.

Arranging the still life
The first consideration when making a still life picture is, of course, the group to be painted or drawn. Care should always be taken to make the arrangement as telling as possible. This does not necessarily mean that it must be full of objects and rhythmic interest, as it may be that an astringent, simple, carefully organized group will possibly hold your interest the better.
Taking the trouble to rearrange the elements several times always repays the painter; taking a different viewpoint or altering the color balance is better done before committing paint to surface, rather than abandoning a half-finished picture.

A few diagrams to demonstrate alternative compositions should be undertaken, and, if one chooses, make a painting of a casual arrangement, such as a table top littered with assorted objects. Edit the final choice by cutting a rectangle to the same proportion to your support in a sheet of stiff white paper and frame the group with it. By holding the frame close to the eye a completely different composition can be seen than that viewed by holding it at arm's length. Experiment with this so that the dialogue between yourself and the subject is allowed full rein. It might well be that by this means one can discover a much better alternative and as well allows unsuspected interpretations by cropping objects or putting things into the fore-

Paul Cézanne, 'Still Life with Teapot'. Cézanne used the still life as a means of experimenting with and expressing his innovative concepts of space and depth. The still life has often been used in such a way since objects are easily arranged to suit the artist's needs. The Cubists carried this idea to its extreme with their revolutionary shattering of space and dimension.

Arranging the still life

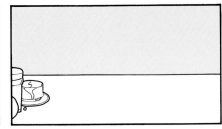

Placement The placement of objects in the picture plane is determined by the emphasis desired by the artist. Left: Objects are centerd to allow the artist to explore their unique and individual qualities. Center: When objects are moved away from the center, interest is created by surrounding the objects with empty space which tends to emphasize, rather than diminish their importance. Right: If too much or too little of the object is shown, the picture can become uninteresting.

Arranging objects The still life can be conveniently altered and rearranged to suit the needs of the artist. Left: Objects have been chosen for their contrasting shapes and the plant in the foreground adds visual interest. Center: A bottle replaces the teapot adding a strong vertical element. The plant is moved further right and downward to allow for the eye to focus on the objects. Right: The plant is included in the group of objects to add contrast in shape and texture.

Drapery Fabrics and drapery are often included in the still life because they offer an interesting textural contrast to the other objects included. For example, a piece of rough sacking is a good counterpoint to either the smooth surface of glass or pottery. Left: Drapery can be used to partially obscure the still life group. Center: The fabric has here been arranged to create a visual direction in the picture; the observer's eye moves from the top, down and around the objects. Right: Placing the fabric in the background can emphasize the still life group.

The figure in still life Left: A picture can contain any number of elements, related or unrelated, and need not be restricted to the traditional still life, portrait, or figure themes. Combining the still life with either a figure or portrait can be extremely interesting and was often used by the masters as a means of demonstrating their skill in all types of subject matter.

ground or lowering eye levels. When the final decision has been taken on the design, color and other components of the group, and the various alternatives have been fully considered, then painting can commence.

Painting techniques
The painting of still life can entail broad generalizations marked in with thin paint with strongly marked details of texture, light and color over-laid; or, especially in watercolor, the quiet selection of tones and color analysed and interpreted in thin, clear washes. Some artists prefer to sketch the main forms in lightly before beginning to paint, others will pour paint on and manipulate it into a scheme. In this, as in so much else, personal experiment will be needed. With practice, the artist will devise the most comfortable and successful process of working.

In pen and ink, still life might prove an interesting subject to interpret in coloured inks rather than simply black and white. Using washes of diluted inks alongside the lines can link up the various parts, especially if those parts are widely spread. Mixing media, perhaps even introducing collage (the application of cut paper to the picture surface) will introduce a fresh approach and suggest further developments.

Vincent Van Gogh,
'Chair and Pipe'.
The still life need
not include only
traditional elements
such as fruit,
flowers, or dishes.
Simple, everyday
objects can be the
subjects for a strong
and interesting
picture.

Oil

IT IS INTERESTING to note in this painting that although the subject is a 'portrait' of peppers and a crab, the theme of the painting is predominantly non-objective. In fact, it is not so much the crab and peppers which determine the strength of the picture but their surroundings which, through the use of color, shape and texture, draws the viewer's attention into the center of the painting.

The environment is made up of flat shapes and planes described in neutral and earth tones which contrast with the roundness of the peppers and crab. Within the wall there are soft, blended tones and strokes which heighten the distinct lines and tones in the subject. The busyness of the checks in the cloth create a visual interest and, again, draw the viewer's eye into the center of the painting while the red cloth creates tension and contrast with the peppers and the stark white background. Note that the red used in the cloth is of a value purposely chosen to avoid overwhelming the rest of the picture with its 'redness' or contrasting too sharply with the green of the peppers.

Materials

Surface
Stretched, primed canvas

Size
35in × 30in (87.5cm × 75cm)

Tools
2B pencil
No 2 sable oil brush
Nos 4, 6 flat bristle brushes
Masking tape

Colors
Black	Cadmium yellow
Burnt sienna	Chrome green
Burnt umber	White
Cadmium red	Yellow ochre

Medium
Turpentine

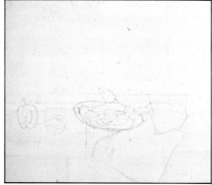

1. With a 2B pencil, lightly put in the shapes and general composition of the painting.

2. Mix white and black and with a No 6 brush block in flat areas of color. With a a No 4 brush and more white, rough in outlines and shadows in the brick wall.

Details · describing cloth · masking tape

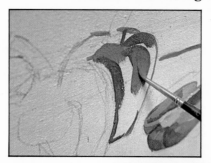

With a small sable brush, the artist works carefully into the shapes using smooth, consistent strokes.

Masking tape is put down over the dried surface; when the shape has been blocked in, the tape is gently pulled away leaving a clean edge.

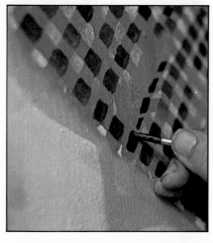

Working over shadow areas in the checked cloth, the artist blocks in squares of pure black with a small sable brush.

6. With black and white, mix shades of grey. Using the No 2 sable brush, paint in squares of cloth using the white of canvas for white squares and light grey for shadow.

7. Work back into the checked cloth with a darker grey and black to strengthen light and dark contrasts.

3. With a No 2 brush and burnt sienna begin to develop the crab. In cadmium red, begin to define the red cloth.

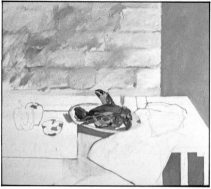

4. Mix chrome green and yellow and with the No 2 brush outline the peppers and put in light areas of color.

5. Mix umber, ochre, and white and block in the table with a No 6 brush. Add a touch of black to cadmium red and develop cloth shadows.

8. Mix white and ochre and lighten background bricks. Use the same grey tone as in the cloth to redefine brick outlines and shadows.

9. Mask the edge of the red cloth with tape and paint over this to create a clean, distinct edge.

10. With the No 2 sable brush and burnt umber, put in horizontal lines in the table and strengthen the shadow area in the table leg.

15

ACRYLICS WERE USED for the under-painting of this picture as they dry much faster than oils and allow the artist to begin to work in oils almost immediately. Note, however, that this process cannot be reversed and oils should not be used as an underpainting for acrylics.

The artist first tinted the canvas with a thin wash of acrylic paint because it is easier to see subtle color tones – especially white – when working on a non-white surface. A purple underpainting was used as a complement to the warm yellows and ochres which, when the underpainting shows through, creates the greenish tone of the finished work.

The color mixtures in this painting are both subtle and sophisticated. While this requires a good sense of color, all were created from the basic colors included in every artist's palette. Unity was achieved throughout the painting by adding small touches of a complementary color to the paint mixtures, such as adding yellow ochre to a predominantly purple tone or cerulean blue to a predominantly orange tone.

Materials

Surface
Stretched and primed canvas

Size
36in × 30in (90cm × 75cm)

Tools
Nos 4, 6 flat bristle brushes
No 2 round sable watercolor brush
Masking tape
Plates or palette
Newspaper or absorbent paper

Acrylic and oil colors
Black	Cobalt blue
Burnt umber	Cobalt purple
Cadmium red medium	Pthalo crimson
Cadmium yellow medium	White
Cerulean blue	Yellow ochre

Mediums
Turpentine
Poppy seed oil
Water

It is important to note that the artist altered the subject halfway through the painting process by exchanging the black boxes and neutral material for a yellow box and green fabric. This was done largely for compositional and interest reasons. The still life artist should feel free to rearrange or alter the subject to suit the painting or drawing.

1. Using acrylic paint, mix a wash of cobalt blue and burnt umber and block in the main outlines and shadow areas with a No 6 bristle brush.

3. Mix black and cobalt blue and put in dark shapes with a No 4 brush. Mix cerulean blue, yellow and white and block in the background.

5. To the above mixture add a small amount of white and cerulean blue. With a No 4 brush begin to describe the highlight areas of the face.

7. Add burnt umber to this mixture and lay in shadow on table. Lighten with white and put in highlight in cloth. Mix cerulean, yellow and put in background.

2. Use thinned pthalo crimson to block in the turban and background. Add cobalt purple for bluish areas. Mix cadmium red and yellow and block in the face and table.

4. With cerulean blue and white, put in light shape on left with a No 6 brush. Mix cadmium red, yellow ochre, and white and block in the light areas beside the head.

6. Mix white, cobalt blue and a small touch of black oil paint and block in the table shape. Add more black to make a darker tone; yellow ochre for warmer areas.

8. Carry the same background tone into the left foreground with a thinner wash of color.

(continued overleaf)

Underpainting · blocking in

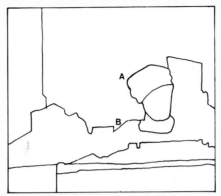

A. With a large brush and thinned acrylic paints, the artist blocks in general color areas scrubbing the paint well into the surface.

B. Once the acrylic underpainting has dried, broad areas of thick, opaque acrylic paint are blocked in.

9. Rework this entire area by painting over previous colors and shapes. Add black to greyish mixture and redefine box shapes with a No 4 brush.

10. Mix white, yellow ochre and a small amount of cerulean blue. With a No 2 sable brush, work in the face highlights with directional strokes.

11. With a thin mixture of permanent magenta and cobalt blue, darken the turban. Carry background color around cast to work around the head.

12. With the same brush and black paint, redraw the box shapes and outlines.

13. With cadmium yellow medium, put in box with a No 4 brush. Use masking tape to create a sharp, clean edge. Using the same yellow, blend into the table area.

14. Using the background tone with cerulean blue added, block in cloth shape to left. Mix white and cerulean blue and apply to the left hand area in even strokes.

15. Mix yellow ochre, burnt umber and white and put in highlights of books to right of case with a No 4 brush. Use same tone for box at left.

16. Add pthalo crimson to white mixture and put in warm tones of face and cloth with a No 2 sable brush.

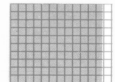

Masking tape · blotting · highlights

If the paint surface should become too wet to work on, a piece of newspaper can be laid over it, gently pressed with the hand, and slowly peeled off. This should not be attempted if the paint is very thick.

With a small sable brush the artist blocks in highlight and shadow areas in the cast. Note the use of the brushstroke to define structure.

Masking tape is a useful tool for creating clean, sharp lines and edges. Here the artist blocks in the box shapes over the tape. The tape is then carefully pulled off the surface.

A PREDOMINANTLY white painting will exercise all of the painter's skills. Preconceived ideas of the effects of color and light must be abandoned in favor of careful and thorough observation. This is thus an excellent way of training your eyes to see the many subtle tones and shades of color which exist in what is commonly believed to be a 'noncolor'.

One way of confronting the problem is to look at the subject in terms of warm and cool color areas. In this painting the white and grey tones are roughly divided between those created from the addition of blue – the cool tones – and those created by the addition of yellow – the warm tones. Until the middle steps of the painting, these warm and cool tones are exaggerated to allow the artist to correct or revise the tones as needed. In the last steps, the entire painting is gradually lightened to allow the subtle color variations to be revealed.

A wide range of marks are achieved by the confident handling of the bristle brushes. The artist has used both the tip and length of the brushes to vary the strokes and textures of the painting.

Materials

Surface
Prepared canvas board

Size
24in × 28in (70cm × 60cm)

Tools
Nos 3, 6 flat bristle brushes
Palette

Colors
Black
Chrome yellow
Cobalt blue
Raw umber
White

Medium
Turpentine

1. Mix a dark grey by adding a little blue to black and white. Thin the paint well with turpentine and sketch in the main areas of the composition with a No 6 brush.

2. Work over the drawing with the tip and flat of the brush, gradually increasing the detail. Aim for a loosely drawn impression of the whole subject.

3. Block in thin layers of paint to show the tonal changes across the image. Start to work over the drawing with thick patches of a lighter blue-grey.

4. With a range of warm and cool greys varied with blue and yellow mixtures, lay in shapes of solid color.

5. Extend the range of tones and build up the complexity of detail. Lighten the colors across the whole image with small dabs and strokes of thick paint.

6. Use the tip of the No 3 brush to draw into the shapes, emphasizing the linear structure and delicacy of the colors.

Outlining · underpainting

The thinned paint is rubbed into the surface – much like a charcoal drawing – to create a variety of tones. This underpainting will be used throughout the painting process to guide the artist in mixing the various shades and hues of white.

The artist is here using the tip of the brush and a very thin grey paint to draw in the basic shapes and composition of the picture.

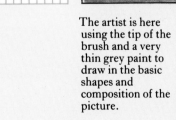

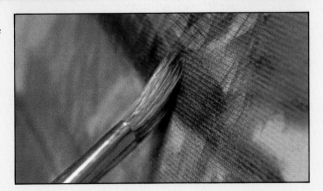

Acrylic

OF THE MANY media and mixed media available to the artist, a prime factor should be which media will most successfully capture the subject. If the painting illustrated were executed in watercolour or pastel rather than acrylic paint, the final effect would be much different. In this case, acrylics were chosen because of the bold colour scheme of the subject. Unlike other painting media, acrylics have an inherent brilliance and brightness which makes them particularly well suited for describing subjects which demand a bold use of color.

In this painting, the aim of the artist was to create a composition using the classical triangle with the wine bottle as a focal point. One of the demands of the still life is that the various objects be arranged in such a way as to avoid flatness in the painting. A mixture of different sizes, shapes, and textures ensures that the finished painting will successfully avoid this problem.

Materials

Surface
Stretched watercolor paper

Size
18in × 14in (45cm × 35cm)

Tools
HB pencil
No 6 flat bristle brush
Nos 2, 4, 6 sable watercolor brushes
Palette

Colors

Alizarin crimson	Hansa orange
Black	Hooker's green
Burnt sienna	Pthalo green
Burnt umber	Violet
Cadmium red medium	White
Cadmium yellow medium	Yellow ochre

Medium
Water

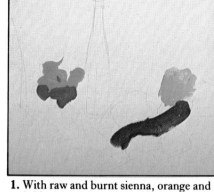

1. With raw and burnt sienna, orange and red, block in shapes in pure color using a No 6 bristle brush

5. Continue across the paper putting in the background. Add a small amount of yellow to the mixture to vary the tone of the green.

For this painting, the consistency of the paint was kept fairly thick and juicy. By adding a matt or gloss medium, the texture may be further altered.

2. Describe green shapes with Hooker's and pthalo green with a No 6 watercolor brush. Vary tones by adding white.

3. Using the same brush and pure white paint, block in the pure white highlight areas of the bottle and cauliflower.

4. Mix a large amount of pthalo green and white and using the No 6 bristle brush, block in the entire background with consistent strokes.

6. Using Hooker's green and a No 4 brush, block in the dark green shadow areas of the background, keeping the paint fairly wet.

7. Add a small amount of burnt sienna to the Hooker's green, and put in shadow areas of foreground.

8. Mix pthalo green and white and with the No 4 brush, describe light areas of the foreground cloth.

(continued overleaf)

Paint consistency · describing shapes · overpainting

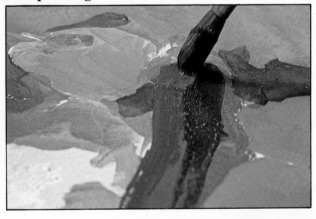

The shape of the eggplant is initially described with broad strokes of light and dark tone.

Shapes of the objects are described with a thinnish mixture of paint and water.

Once the underpainting has dried thoroughly, a thick layer of paint is laid down.

Detailing and highlights

Highlights within
the bunch of
radishes are created
by using a strong
red.

A juicy mixture of
white and yellow
ochre is used to
describe cauliflower
florets.

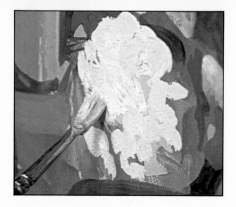

9. Carry this same light green tone into the background area.

Using a pale green tone similar to that in the background, the artist here puts in the finishing touches on the eggplant.

10. With a No 2 brush and Hooker's green, put in the dark shadow areas of the green vegetables. With the same brush and pure white, put in highlights.

11. With pure white and the No 2 brush, block in cauliflower. Put in strong highlights in white in the bottle.

Highlights can be created by using pure white paint directly from the tube.

12. Mix pthalo green and white and with the same brush, put in the beans with fluid, even strokes.

ALTHOUGH ACRYLIC paints were used for this painting, the method is an extremely old oil technique used by the masters for hundreds of years. Through sophisticated means of investigation, art historians have been able to cut through the hundreds of years of wear and tear inflicted upon these paintings, down to the original surface. In so doing, the actual progression of the painting has been revealed. The masters would first develop an extensive underpainting – sometimes as detailed and carefully rendered as the finished painting. The dark underpainting meant that the artist was required to work from dark to light, rather than vice versa. Layer upon layer of thin washes of color were put one upon the other, slowly building up a translucent and shimmering surface. This was a slow and painstaking process, made much more efficient by the introduction of acrylic paints in this century.

Using this traditional method, the artist has here worked on a tinted ground, painting from dark to light with very thin layers of color. The dark underpainting ensures a unity in the painting as it permeates all subsequent layers of paint giving an overall warmth.

Before beginning to paint, the artist carefully arranged the subject and then drew a comprehensive sketch of what the painting would consist of. This allowed him to complete the picture rapidly once begun, as all preliminary planning and decision-making had been finished beforehand.

Materials

Surface
Prepared canvas board

Size
16in × 20in (40cm × 50cm)

Tools
2B pencil
Nos 2, 4, 10 sable round oil brushes
Rags or tissues
Plates or palette

Colors
Black
Burnt umber
Cadmium yellow light
White
Yellow ochre

Medium
Water

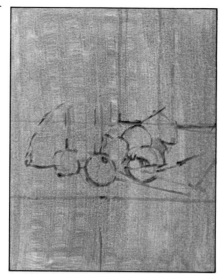

1. After the underpainting has dried, sketch in the subject with a 2B pencil. Work over this with thin black paint and a No 2 brush.

2. With a thin mixture of white and water, block in the lightest areas of the painting with a No 10 brush. Blend with a brush, finger, or rag.

4. When dry, use a No 4 brush and pure white working over the entire surface, blocking in strong highlight areas.

5. With a No 2 sable brush, redraw subject outlines in black thinned with water.

7. With a thinnish mixture of black and water, strengthen shadow areas around onions and table.

8. Apply a thin wash of white and yellow ochre over the foreground table area and background with a No 10 brush. Work well into the surface.

Washes of color · highlighting

3. Darken the umber tone by adding more paint and start to put in the darkest areas of the painting working the paint well into the surface.

6. Mix white, cadmium yellow and water and with the No 2 brush put in the highlight areas of the onions. With pure white put in cloth highlights.

9. Mix white and black in a lightish tone and rework highlights and reflections in the bottle with a No 2 brush.

After the underpainting has dried thoroughly, the artist blocks in broad areas of white thinned with water.

With a thin wash of yellow ochre and water, the artist is here blocking in the yellow tone of the onions.

With a fine brush and white paint, the artist develops the texture of the paper beside the milk bottle.

THIS STILL LIFE was deliberately arranged as a study of warm and cool color contrasts and is composed of simple, strong shapes. Each object has a predominant color 'temperature' to show fresh, cool color against a glowing hot tone. This mutually-enhancing use of complementary color is heightened by small touches of shadow which, again, are treated as color contrasts rather than dark tones.

As it is difficult to determine the effects of color relationships in advance, the artist must work by a continual process of adjustment, watching the development of the painting as carefully as he observes the subject.

The acrylic paint is applied thickly, layer upon layer. Overpaint in broad areas of color leaving small broken shapes of underpainting showing through. The overall effect will be lessened if the paint is too thin, so add only enough water to make it workable and use flat brushes to obtain an even, opaque surface.

Materials

Surface
Prepared canvas board

Size
16in × 14in (40cm × 35cm)

Tools
Nos 2, 3, 5 flat bristle brushes
No 6 flat synthetic brush
Plate or palette

Colors

Alizarin crimson	Chrome green
Black	Chrome orange
Cadmium lemon	Cobalt blue
Cadmium red	Ultramarine blue
Cadmium yellow	Violet

Medium
Water

1. Outline the shapes of the fruit and paper in red with a bristle brush and lay in shadows. Work over the background with a light grey tone.

3. Work on the two apples developing the tonal structure to show the rounded forms. Darken the tone of the shadows with a strong blue-black.

5. Exaggerate the colors to develop the interplay of complementary hues, showing shadows and highlights as bright, pure color.

7. Treat the red apple with touches of blue shadow to show the contours. Lighten the tones of the green apple and the foreground and background colors.

2. Block in each shape with its local color in a thick, flat layer and brush.

4. Put in red and green tones in the orange and build up the contrast of color over all the shapes. Lighten the blues and purples of the table top and the background tone.

6. Work over the orange and lemon with flat areas of local color leavingg blue, green, and violet shadows to describe the rounded forms and the fall of light.

8. Add small details in the shapes and colors over the whole image, adjusting the contrasts and refining the outlines.

Outlining in red · background · blocking in shapes

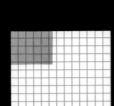

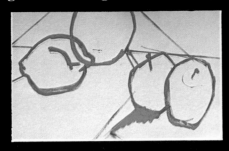

The artist first describes outlines and shadow areas in a strong red tone. Red was chosen as a complement to the final colors used.

Working around the outlines of the fruit, the artist is here blocking in the background.

With a thick, well-mixed orange tone, the artist blocks in the main color areas.

Watercolor

THE STRUCTURE OF this painting depends upon the development of negative shapes, that is, the spaces between the objects rather than the objects themselves. The image is built up as a jigsaw pattern of small patches of color which are brought together in the final stages of the painting. This is a useful approach in any media; however, with watercolor, you must be precise from the start as it is too transparent to be heavily corrected.

The painting is small and loosely described and thus you will not need a large range of brushes or colors. Lay in broad washes of color with a loaded brush, letting the bristles spread; draw the hairs to a fine point to describe small shapes and linear details. The whole painting should be allowed to dry frequently so the layers of color stay clear and separate, building up gradually to their full intensity. Balance the contrast of warm and cool tones with the hot reds and yellows of the chairs standing out from the cooler tones of the green and blue background.

Dark patches of color can be lightened by gently rubbing over them with a clean, wet Q-tip, but try to keep corrections to a minimum or the surface may be damaged. When the image is completely dry, work over the shapes with colored pencils. This modifies the colors and adds a grainy texture to the flat washes.

Materials

Surface
Stretched cartridge paper

Size
14in × 11.5in (35cm × 29cm)

Tools
HB pencil
Nos 3, 6 round sable brushes

Colors
Burnt sienna	Ultramarine
Cadmium yellow medium	Violet
Emerald green	Yellow ochre
Prussian blue	

Medium
Water

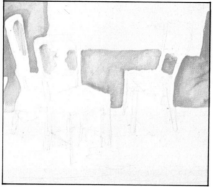

1. Very lightly draw up the shapes with an HB pencil. Work into the background with washes of burnt sienna, Prussian blue, yellow ochre and violet with a No 6 brush.

2. Move across the painting laying in patches of thin color. Add emerald green and viridian to the range of colors.

3. Develop color contrasts by working into the shape of the chairs with yellow, red and orange and intensifying the blue and green of the background.

4. Give the shadows on the chairs and floor depth with touches of blue and violet.

5. Draw into the shapes with the tip of the No 3 brush to clarify linear structure. Darken the background to heighten the outline of the chairs.

Describing shapes · colored pencils

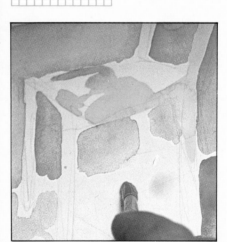

Here the chair shapes are created by the artist by describing the space around the shapes and leaving the paper bare to describe the chairs.

After the painting is thoroughly dry, colored pencils are used to strengthen shadows and color tones. Do not press too hard as the paper will be fragile due to the paint layer.

THE FRESHNESS of watercolor depends upon the gradual building up from light to dark and any attempt to create highlights or pale tones in the final stages of the painting will alter the entire character of the medium. Accuracy is thus all-important in the initial structuring of the composition. White shapes must be precise and clean, created 'negatively' by careful drawing of surrounding color areas.

A light pencil sketch will help to establish the correct proportions, but complex shapes are outlined directly with a fine sable brush. Block in solid colors quickly or a hard line will appear around the edges of the shapes. Use large brushes to work into the foreground and background and lightly spatter paint dripped from the end of a large brush to create a mottled texture.

A limited range of color was used, mixing in black to create dark tones and varying greys with small touches of red and blue. Dry the painting frequently so that colors remain separate and the full range of tone and texture emerges through overlaid washes.

Materials

__Surface__
Stretched cartridge paper

__Size__
16in × 22.5in (40cm × 57cm)

__Tools__
Nos 2, 5 sable round watercolor brushes
No 12 ox-ear flat brush
1in (2.5cm) decorators' brush

__Colors__
Black	Payne's grey
Burnt sienna	Ultramarine
Burnt umber	Vermilion
Cobalt blue	Yellow ochre

__Medium__
Water

1. Draw the basic shapes of the objects in outline with a pencil. Mix a very thin wash of Payne's grey and block in the whole of the background.

3. Mix a light brown from red and black and work over the red, showing folds and creases in the fabric and dark shadows. Lay a wash of brown across foreground.

5. Strengthen all the colors, breaking up the shapes into small tonal areas. Bring out textural details by overlaying washes and spattering the paint lightly.

2. Paint in the local colors of the objects building up the paint in thin layers and leaving white space to show highlights and small details. Keep each color separate.

4. Work up shadows in the blue in the same way using a mixture of blue and black. Move over the whole painting putting in dark tones.

6. Intensify the dark brown in the foreground and use the same brown to indicate shadow on the wall behind. Vary the strength of the color.

Negative shapes · spattering

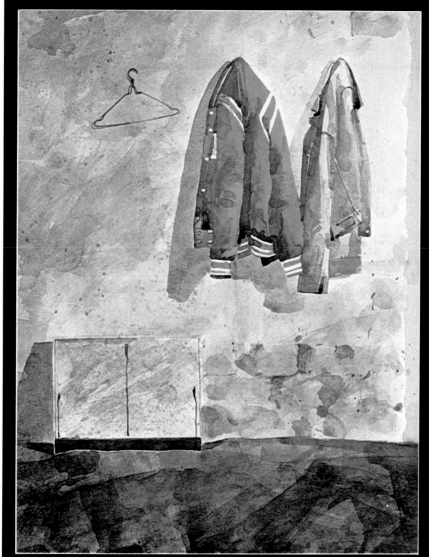

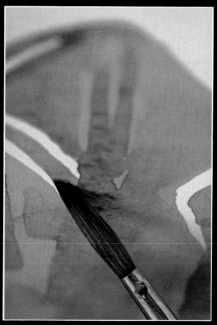

A good example of the use of negative shapes. Here the artist creates the white lines in the jacket by describing the red areas around them rather than by painting the lines.

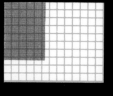

Spattering to create texture. Using a decorator's brush, the artist holds the brush above the paper and taps it lightly to create a tonal effect.

THE ARTIST can learn as much, if not more, from working with a limited palette and simple subject as he can from using many colors and a complicated subject.

This type of painting can be more difficult than painting on a large or complex scale as the artist is required to study carefully the subject in order to see minute variations in shape, tone, and color. You will discover that shadows are not merely areas of grey, but include very slight color differentiations and barely perceptible variations in tone. You will see how a simple piece of lettuce – which most people would describe as 'leafy green' – is in reality made up of many colors, tiny veins of light, and reflections.

An interesting experiment is to make the subject larger than real life. This type of work takes great concentration but the rewards are many. You will find that when you move on to more complex subjects, you will use what you have learned while working in detail on simple subjects.

Materials

Surface
Watercolor pad

Size
10in × 12in (25cm × 30cm)

Tools
No 2 sable watercolor brush
Plate or palette

Colors
Light red
Ultramarine blue
Viridian green
Yellow ochre

Medium
Water

1. Draw in the design with a No 2 sable brush and ultramarine blue.

2. Using just enough water to keep the paint flowing, develop a small area of the picture and then carry this color over to a new area.

Finished picture · outlining · working in new area

To finish off the picture (right), the artist laid a blue wash around the left side, running over and into the lettuce shape. This served to heighten blue tones within the lettuce and contrast with the red outside.

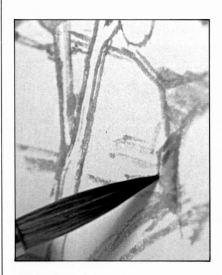

With a fine point sable brush, the artist begins by working over the preliminary pencil sketch with a thin wash of blue.

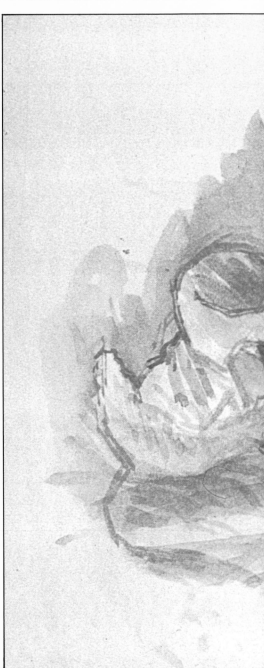

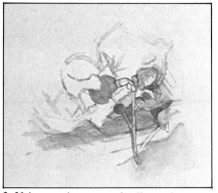

3. Using varying tones of yellow ochre, light red, viridian, and blue, work over the entire picture. Work back and forth between new and old areas.

4. Working into the outlined area with a wash of greens, develop a contrast between the lettuce and other leaves with different shades of green.

5. Strengthen outlines in blue and red. The red outline contrasts with the predominant blues and greens of the subject. Leave the white of the paper.

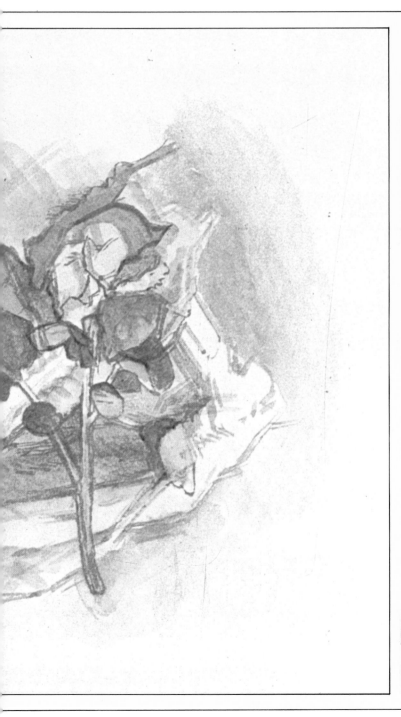

The artist worked in small areas, one at a time. Here the completed area can be seen and the artist is now describing the blue outline for the next area to be painted.

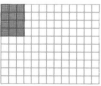

IT IS NOT always necessary to go to great lengths to assemble a still life as a small, ordinary object such as a teabag offers a complex structure and intricate range of tones and colors. As well, practice in quick watercolor studies develops keen perception and skills in drawing and painting which are a sound basis for work in any medium.

Here watercolor is used for a study which is essentially direct and immediate. The painting is rapidly completed, building up the form with a combination of line and thin washes of paint; the subject emerges through a careful interpretation of tiny shapes of color and tone.

In small paintings of this kind, the paint should be wet but not overly so, ensuring that the marks are easy and fluid but controlled. The final effect is achieved by constantly checking lines and shapes; working wash over line; and drawing back into the washes. A limited range of color is used to create a variety of tones, demonstrating the rich versatility and potential of watercolors.

Materials

Surface
Cartridge paper

Size
7in × 10in (17cm × 25cm)

Tools
No 2 round watercolor brush

Colors
Black	Prussian blue
Cobalt blue	Viridian
Light red	Yellow ochre

Medium
Water

1. Load the brush with Prussian blue paint, well thinned with water. Draw the outline of the shape and details of the form with the point of the brush.

2. Block in shadow areas with thin washes of cobalt blue. The color should not be too too strong as this is the basis of a series of overlaid layers of paint.

3. Let the painting dry and then start to define the shapes with washes of light red. Overlay red on blue to bring out the form.

4. Continue to work with light red, cooling the tone where necessary with yellow ochre. Add definition to the shadows with blue washes in and around the outlines.

5. Draw into the washes of paint with a stronger tone of light red to describe creases in the surface. Indicate the shape of the plate with a light wash of viridian.

6. Where the color is too strong, lighten with a brush dipped in clean water. When the surface is dry, draw up the outlines again in blue with the point of the brush.

Initial washes · redefining outlines

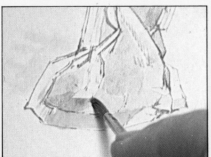

After the initial outlines have been described, the artist begins to put in a very thin wash of color using the tip of the brush.

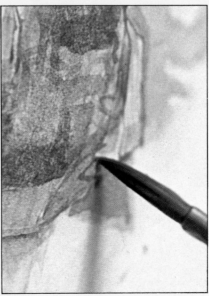

The blue outline is used over and over again in the painting process to strengthen shape and contrast.

Gouache

GOUACHE IS a water-based paint but thicker and more opaque than water-color. The colors are clear and bright; mixed with white they create sparkling pastel tints. Use thick paint straight from the tube to overlay strong colors, or thin it with water to flood in light washes.

At first glance this painting may appear to be carefully detailed and realistic but, as the steps show, the technique is fluid and informal. The first step, for example, is not a meticulous drawing but a mass of vivid, liquid pools of color suggesting basic forms. As the paint is laid on in layers of loose streaks and patches, the impression of solidity and texture gradually emerges. Each object is described by carefully studying the subject colors and translating these into the painting.

In general, the technique used for this painting was to thicken the paint slightly with each application; but thin washes are laid in the final stage to indicate textures and shadows. The combination of thin washes with flat, opaque patches of color is most effective in capturing the reflective surface of the bottle and glass.

Materials

__Surface__
Stretched cartridge paper

__Size__
12.5in × 17in (31cm × 45cm)

__Tools__
No 12 flat ox-ear brush
Nos 5, 8 round sable brushes
Plate or palette

__Colors__
Burnt umber   Sap green
Cadmium yellow   Yellow ochre
Magenta   White

__Medium__
Water

1. With a No 8 sable brush lay in the basic shapes of the objects with thin, wet paint. Use burnt umber, sap green, magenta and yellow and let the color flow together.

2. With a No 5 brush, put in yellow ochre around the shapes and into the foreground. Work over the bottle and loaf of bread, painting in shadow details.

3. Indicate shadows in the background with a thin layer of green. Apply small patches of solid color to show form and surface texture in each object.

4. With a No 12 brush, block in small dabs and streaks of color, developing the tones and textures.

5. Intensify the contrast of light and dark with white highlights and brown shadows with the No 5 brush. Work into the background with white.

6. Work over the foreground and background with light tones of pink and yellow, keeping the paint thin. Spatter brown and black over the loaf.

Painting wet-in wet · overpainting dry surface · using paint from tube

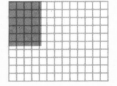

A. After dampening the paper in the shape of the object with water, the artist lays in a wash of color, allowing it to bleed over the damp area.

B. Over the dry underpainting, the artist here blocks in the label on the bottle with dryish paint.

C. Using paint directly from the tube and a large brush well loaded with water, the background is blocked in.

Tempera

WITH A small surface and tempera paints, the artist can create a finished painting in a very short period of time. While the medium can be used with virtually any sized surface or type of subject, it is particularly well suited to small working areas and finely detailed work. To create this picture, the artist worked on a small piece of hardboard, with the finished work resembling a miniature or enamelled tile.

The scratching-back technique can give a tempera painting textural interest. Although tempera dries to a sticky state fairly quickly, it remains workable for a short period of time. Scratching-back the surface with a sharp object to the original color of the paper or board and either leaving it or reglazing it will add luminosity and allow the artist to develop fine details. This process can be carried on almost indefinitely.

Pure, dry pigments can be very expensive, especially the inorganic colors such as the blues and reds, but it is worth acquiring some and experimenting with the true tempera technique. On the other hand, it is perfectly acceptable to use commercial watercolors in tubes and mix these with a yolk medium for a less expensive method of tempera painting.

Materials

Surface
Primed hardboard

Size
6in × 7.5in (15cm × 19cm)

Tools
HB pencil
Nos 2, 4 sable watercolor brushes
Knife or scalpel

Dry pigment colors
Black
Burnt umber   Cobalt blue
Cadmium green   Yellow ochre
Cadmium red

Mediums
Egg yolk
Water

1. With fine sandpaper, sand a primed board until smooth. Put in the initial sketch with an HB pencil and sand again.

2. With a No 2 sable brush, mix egg yolk with yellow ochre and put in the skull with short, vertical strokes. Do the same in cadmium red for the flowers.

3. Mix cerulean blue and yolk and, with a No 4 brush, put in the background. Add a touch of black and put in the shadow areas of the table.

4. With more cerulean blue, block in the vase. Develop the shadows of the skull in burnt umber.

5. Mix black and cerulean blue in a darker tone and work back into the shadow areas with the No 2 brush.

6. With a sharp tool, scratch back the paint surface in the highlight areas, hatching with the point. Brush burrs of paint away with a rag or tissue.

Creating texture and tone

To create an interesting textural effect, the artist is here seen scratching through the paint layer with a sharp knife. Fine lines can be drawn through the paint and crosshatched to create texture and tone. The paint surface should be tacky, not dry.

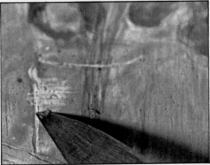

Pastel

THE STILL life can be an excellent way for the artist to explore various media and experiment with different ways of seeing. The choice of objects and their arrangement is virtually infinite; the artist can pick and choose and arrange his subject to suit every need.

In this pastel, the artist chose to work with simple objects and a few bold colors. While this may at first seem the easier course to take – as opposed to complex subject matter and color schemes – to work with a few primary colors and a simple subject can often be a very difficult task. The main problem in working with bold colors is how to control their intensities so that one does not overpower the other. Although tones and hues may be altered and adjusted by blending, to retain the freshness and vibrancy of the individual colors demands that the artist carefully balance and weigh individual color areas. One way to ensure a balanced picture is to introduce a complementary color into a general color area. Thus in this picture there are small strokes of red within predominantly blue areas, and vice versa. This will also help to give the picture unity, as the observer's eye will pick up the individual colors as it moves around the picture.

Materials

Surface
Pastel paper

Size
18.5in × 26in (46cm × 65cm)

Tools
HB pencil or willow charcoal
Tissues or rags
Fixative

Colors
Blue-green	Pale blue
Cobalt blue	Pink
Red	Prussian blue
Green	Yellow
Orange	

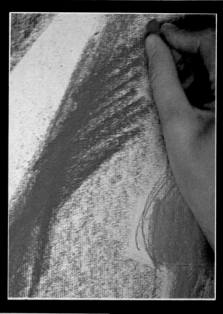

After the initial areas of color have been laid down, the artist works back over these to strengthen tones.

Overlaying thin strokes of pure color will create an optical color mixture on the drawing surface.

1. After lightly sketching the subject in with pencil, use the side of the chalk to put in the main color areas in blue, green, and orange.

2. Using the end of the chalk, begin to work up stronger colors with sharp, directional strokes.

Finished picture · strengthening tones · mixing color · textures

The finished picture shows a skilful handling of strong primary colors to create a balanced and dynamic image. Compositionally, the use of forceful diagonals adds to the overall vitality of the picture.

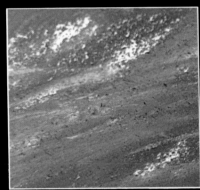

The surface texture is clearly seen in this picture; dense areas of color are mixed with white gaps in the paper to create a gradated effect.

3. Begin to describe lights and darks in green areas by using various tones of green. Carry the red tone into the blue of the backdrop.

4. Intensify dark areas with dark green, Prussian blue, and dark red.

5. With pale blue, work into the foreground area as a highlight and tone down the background with the same color.

ARTISTS WHO experiment with oil pastels quickly grasp their potential for producing strong, brilliant pictures. They are an extremely flexible medium and can be used either like traditional chalk pastels in thin layers of color, or painted on to the surface by softening them with turpentine and applying them with a palette knife.

The picture shown here illustrates the intensity and brilliance characteristic of oil pastels in creating an interesting and dramatic picture. They are best suited to bold, colorful work, although it is just as possible to work with subtle overlays of color. There is a possibility of the surface being built up too quickly, but the artist can always scratch back into the pastel with a sharp tool to either clean up the surface or draw in fine lines of detail.

The composition of this drawing is particularly striking in its use of strong shapes, colors, and the clean white space of the paper. The lack of any additional background information in no way detracts from the forcefulness of the image and, if anything, causes the subject to stand out in bold relief.

Materials

__Surface__
Rough, heavyweight drawing paper

__Size__
21in × 23in (52cm × 57.5cm)

__Tools__
HB pencil

__Colors__

Black	Medium red
Dark blue	Pink
Green	Yellow

1. Lightly sketch in the subject with an HB pencil.

2. With a medium red pastel, work over the jacket outlines and block in red with light, broad strokes.

3. With dark blue, rough in the shadow areas with light strokes.

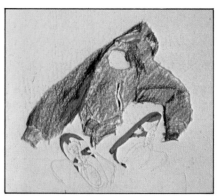

4. With a medium yellow, put in the trim on the jacket. With the same red as before, put in the red of the shoes. Do the same with a green pastel.

5. With medium yellow, block in the rest of the shoe color, pressing the pastel hard into the surface.

6. Work back into the jacket with the medium red, bearing hard against the surface. Rework the shadow areas with the same pressure.

7. Continue the previous step until the entire jacket area is covered.

8. Work over the red in the jacket with deep blue, strengthening shadow areas. With a pink pastel, put in highlights in the jacket.

Color areas · developing the picture

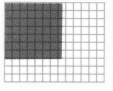

The artist begins by roughing in the basic color areas using a light, sweeping motion.

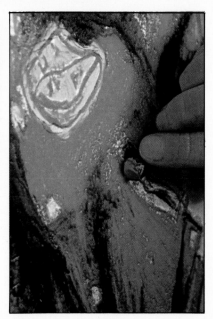

With each subsequent layer of color, the pastel is pressed more firmly on to the surface to fill the tiny white gaps in the paper grain.

A STILL LIFE need not consist only of the usual subjects such as fruits, glasses and drapery. It is possible to take very ordinary, everyday objects and interpret them in such a way as to create an interesting and stimulating image.

The picture shown here is a good example of the artist taking a subject and, through the use of exaggeration, innovation and careful observation, creating an individual interpretation of a basically commonplace object. The subject was chosen for its lack of color. On first glance, the viewer sees only tones of grey and white; however, on careful observation it becomes apparent that within these general color areas are myriads of subtle colors and tones. Very slight and subtle color variations were discovered within the subject which were emphasized and exaggerated, Thus, where the white of the tiles turns into a coolish blue, the artist described this in much stronger blues and purples; where the tone turns warmer and pinker, a strong orange or red are used.

This method of drawing – exaggerating what is seen – not only helps the artist understand color. It also trains the eye to look for hidden tones and subtle nuances of hue.

Materials

Surface
Blue pastel paper

Size
18.5in × 26in (46cm × 65cm)

Tools
HB pencil
Tissues or rags
Fixative

Colors
Blue-green	Light orange
Cadmium red	Light yellow
Cerulean blue	Orange
Cobalt blue	Pale blue
Light green	Prussian blue

1. After sketching in the subject roughly in pencil, use the side of the pastel to put in broad color areas of white, yellow, and cerulean blue.

2. Blend these areas with a small piece of tissue. With orange, overlay the warmer color areas. With red chalk, draw in the outlines of the tiles in the floor and wall.

3. Using pale blue and light green, begin to develop the cooler, shadow areas in the tiles. Carry red and orange tones over the rest of the picture.

Developing details

Here the artist uses the end of a piece of red pastel to describe the red line above the tiles. A combination of such techniques – strong linear strokes and soft blending – add interest to the overall image.

4. Lay in red, pink and orange over blue areas to create purplish tones. Begin to put in warm tile colors in yellow and orange.

5. Put in pale green strip on right and in the tiles. Strengthen red and blue strips to the left.

6. Overlay white area above the sink with light orange and yellow and blend with fingers or tissue.

Pencil

A STILL LIFE arrangement can be an excellent vehicle for the study of color, shape, and structure. The still life may take any form from the traditional subject of fruit and flowers to a jumble of objects randomly selected from whatever is at hand. Choose objects which offer an interesting pattern of forms; develop contrasts and harmonies in the range of colors and between geometric and irregular shapes.

The final effect of this drawing is created by successive overlaying of lines in different colors, woven together to create a range of subtle hues. Each layer is described by lightly hatching and crosshatching to gradually build up the overall effect. Blue and purple form rich, deep shadows in the yellows; a light layer of red over yellow warms up the basic color without overpowering its character.

Materials

Surface
Cartridge paper

Size
23in × 23in (57cm × 57cm)

Tools
HB pencil

Colored pencils
Black	Purple
Burnt sienna	Scarlet
Burnt umber	Ultramarine blue
Cobalt blue	Yellow
Grey	Yellow ochre

Finished picture · describing details · overlaying color

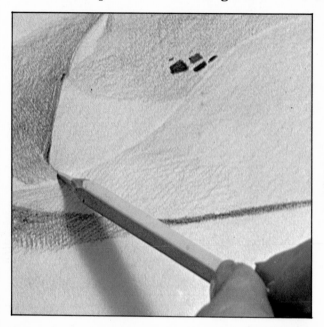

The finished picture (right) illustrates how colored pencil may be used to create a subtle, atmospheric image. The combination of soft tones with a strong composition create a balanced and interesting image.

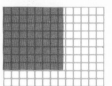

Subtle color tones are created by overlaying light strokes of color. Here the artist works over a shadow area with a light yellow pencil.

Small detail areas are described with a dark pencil. This is sharpened to a fine point.

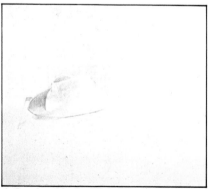

1. Lay in a block of light blue shading behind the hat, varying the direction of the pencil strokes. Use the same blue for shadows on and around the hat.

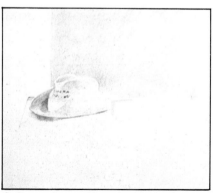

2. Strengthen and broaden the background color. Develop the shadows and pattern details of the hat. Draw in the shape of the boxes with yellow and red pencils.

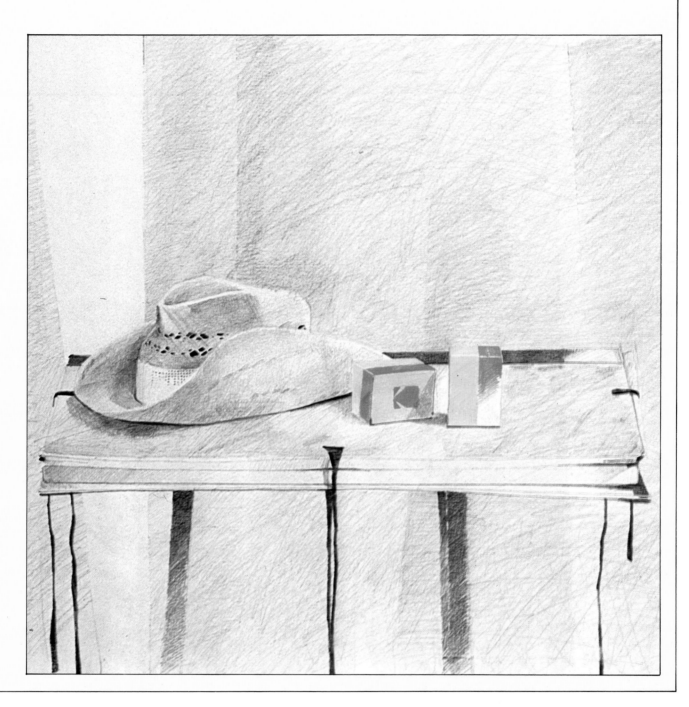

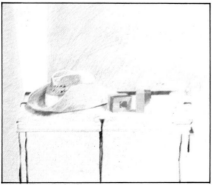

3. Build up the colors with contrasts of tone. Use purple in shadows under the hat, and darken blues to make the objects stand out from the background.

4. Outline the portfolio and sketchbook in black. Strengthen the bright colors against the neutral greys.

5. Lay in the rest of the background area in blue and vary the tones by heavily reworking. Build up details of line and tone with black and yellow ochre.

MANY OF THE products of graphic designers are the inspiration for still life paintings. There are any number of designs and patterns, bright colors and vivid images, all deliberately designed to be eye-catching, which the artist can exploit to create a stunning painting or drawing.

Any technique which aims to reproduce a detailed surface pattern demands patience and precision. Because the colors used in packaging tend to be intense and artificial, the bright colors of colored pencils are well suited to this type of subject matter.

The colors are solidly blocked in with heavy shading with patterns following curves, angles, and reflections of the objects. These factors all serve to modify the shapes and tones.

Because the image is complex, it is best to draw every detail first with an ordinary pencil. Graphite pencil is more easily erased than colored pencil, so all corrections can be made before the color is applied. Keep the outlines light, and follow them closely when blocking in the color.

Materials

Surface
Cartridge paper

Size
20in × 24in (50cm × 60cm)

Tools
HB pencil
Putty eraser

Colors

Black	Purple
Dark green	Scarlet
Emerald green	Yellow
Magenta	Yellow ochre

1. Draw up the still life in outline with an HB pencil. Work on each shape in detail to show the surface designs.

2. Start to work into one shape in color. Thicken the outline of the lettering with a black pencil and shade in the colored patterns with green and yellow-brown.

3. Continue to build up the color, working with solid shapes and heavy lines.

4. Work over another shape with thick red, following the pencil outlines precisely and shading in all directions.

5. Gradually extend the color across the drawing. Describe the patterns exactly as they appear on each object.

6. Draw into each shape in the drawing in turn, developing the color and completing the patterning.

Shadow areas

Using a sharpened pencil, the artist works back into color areas to create darker tones. The shape of the tins is largely created by this gradation of tone.

THIS PICTURE illustrates how willow charcoal, although a fragile medium, can create a very dramatic finished drawing. The drawing process was one of working up dark areas and then modifying them with a putty eraser to achieve a balance between light and shadow. There is a constant movement between the building up of dark areas, lightening them, and then working back into the shadow areas – and then repeating the entire process.

In all drawing media, and particularly with charcoal, it is to your advantage to experiment with the various textures and tones the medium is capable of producing. From a very fine, fluid line to a heavy and dense black, charcoal is flexible enough to fulfil every creative need. Because it is so easily erased, artists feel comfortable with willow charcoal. Where it can be difficult to lay down strong paint colours, with charcoal the artist can let his imagination run free without fear of spoiling a picture, as any mistake is easily corrected or altered.

Materials

Surface
Cartridge paper

Size
20in × 24in (50cm × 60cm)

Tools
Light and medium willow charcoal
Putty eraser
Tissues
Fixative

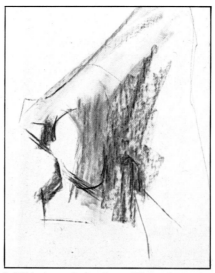

1. With the end of a piece of light charcoal, rough in the general shapes. Using the side of the stick, begin to block in the various shadow areas.

2. Blend charcoal over the face and draw in the features. Strengthen outlines with a heavy line.

3. With a putty eraser, erase out highlight areas in cast and fabric.

4. With medium charcoal, put in shape and shadows in the fabric and the area around the head. Draw in the outline of the fabric and the table.

5. Work back into the head using the side of a piece of light charcoal. Blend with a piece of rag or a finger.

6. Blend the background shadow. With the putty eraser, lighten all shadows by lightly drawing the eraser across the surface.

Finished picture · facial details · using a putty eraser

The attractive qualities of using willow charcoal are shown in the finished picture. By a skilful handling of tone and texture, the artist has produced an unusual still life. Note in particular the combination of different textures and shapes to add visual interest.

Here the artist puts in dark facial details using the tip of the charcoal.

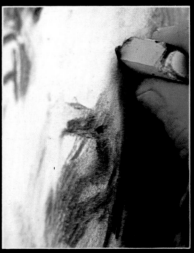

By using a putty eraser, the artist can erase back through the charcoal layer to create highlights and subtle tones of grey.

Pen and ink

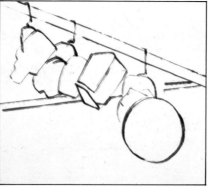

1. Sketch in the outline of the shapes with a pencil to establish the basic positions. Using this drawing as a guide, work with a thick-nibbed pen to define the main shapes.

2. Work boldly in line, drawing into the objects in more detail.

PEN AND INK is a bold, direct drawing medium and therefore demands a degree of confidence in its user. The drawing must be clearly defined through careful observation of the subject and strong interpretation on to the drawing surface. Describe the shapes and contours of each object and use surface detail only where it clarifies and adds texture to the form.

The composition can be sketched out lightly in pencil at the start to establish proportions and relationships of the objects. This should only be a light guideline since the aim is not to trace over the pencil drawing with ink, but to fulfil the medium's potential through direct drawing. Vary the line quality by using thick and thin nibs and so distinguish between solid, hard-edged objects and fine, linear details.

Any initial errors in the drawing can provide a structure on which to more boldly and accurately develop the image. Unwanted marks can be removed by painting over them with a thin layer of white gouache. When this is dry, the shapes can be redrawn in ink. The paint must be applied sparingly as the ink will not work over thick paint and the drawing loses vitality if corrections are too heavy.

Materials

Surface
Thick cartridge paper

Size
25in × 18in (62cm × 45cm)

Tools
Pen holder
Large, square nib
Small mapping pen
No 5 round sable brush

Colors
Black waterproof India ink
White designers' gouache

Medium
Water

With a fine nibbed pen, the artist works back over the initial pen sketch, darkening and broadening outlines.

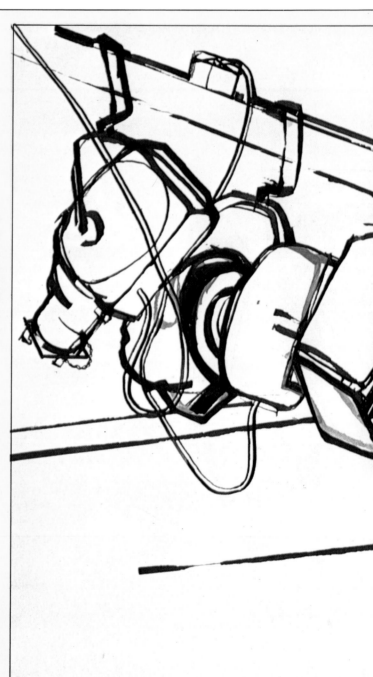

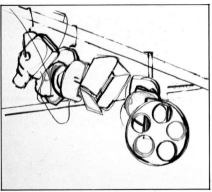

3. Continue to add detail and correct the basic shapes, building up a dense network of lines. Use a fine mapping pen to vary the texture.

4. Take out incorrect lines by painting them over with white gouache. Keep the paint thin so that ink can be applied over it later on during the drawing.

5. Pick out areas of dark tone and pattern with heavy strokes of the broad nib. Keep a balance between plain and patterned areas, thick and fine lines.

Redefining outlines · using white gouache

White designer's gouache is mixed with a small amount of water in a dish. With a small sable brush, the artist paints out unwanted lines of ink. Once thoroughly dry, the gouache can be worked over again with the pen.

WHILE IT IS possible to describe a subject with accuracy and precision, a picture often needs some creative license to make it more interesting. In this case, the artist has taken the general shape, composition, and color of the subject and through an individual use of line and color washes has exaggerated features to make the picture more descriptive. The techniques used are washed-in color, line, and crosshatching, juxtaposed to create an interesting combination of textures.

One important aspect of this drawing is the use of negative space to define details. In the finished picture, the laces outside of the boot have been created by the use of line. Moving on to the boot's surface, it is the area of colored wash surrounding the white of the paper which continues the image of the lace rather than the pen line itself.

Materials

Surface
Cartridge paper

Size
15in × 22in (38cm × 58cm)

Tools
Pen holder
Small nib
No 2 sable brush
Palette

Ink colors
Black waterproof India ink
Burnt sienna
Red

Medium
Water

1. Begin to put in the outline, varying the line by moving the pen both quickly and slowly. Dip a brush in water and let the pen line bleed into that wet area.

3. Mix a small amount of red and burnt sienna and work into the other boot. With pen and black ink, rework the outline of the boot allowing the ink to run .

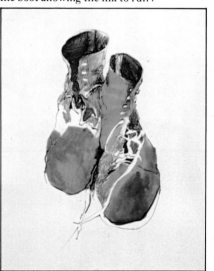

5. Using the pen and black ink, work back into the shoe with crosshatching strokes to create the area around the laces.

2. Carry the outline further down using red ink. Begin to create shadow textures within the boot with the same red, applied in directional strokes.

4. With mixture of red and black ink, crosshatch in the remaining white area of the right boot, leaving parts of the surface untouched to create laces and holes.

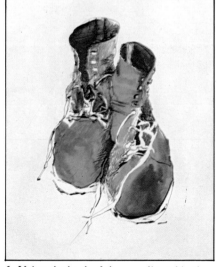

6. Using the back of the pen dipped in the black ink, roughly describe the sole of the boots.

Finished picture · preliminary wash · back of pen · negative space and line

The artists completed the picture by laying a darker wash over shadow areas in the left shoe.

The preliminary wash is put in and will later be worked over with pen and ink.

Using negative space to describe shape, the artist uses a hatched tone to create a white area.

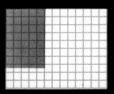

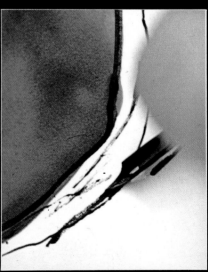

By turning the pen on its back, the artist is able to create a rough, jagged line.

ALTHOUGH THE rapidograph is used largely by the commercial artist, it has gained popularity with the fine-artist as well.

As a drawing tool, the instrument has advantages and disadvantages. On the positive side, the artist need not constantly stop to dip the pen in ink, as the reservoir inside the rapidograph provides a constant source. The rapidograph line tends to be more consistent and even than the traditional pen and ink, and less apt to blot. On the negative side, the rapidograph can be finicky and temperamental. The pen must be kept in a near-upright position while drawing and frequently shaken to keep the ink flowing. The line produced is fine and descriptive, but the artist must first acquire a sensitive touch to obtain this effect.

While the drawing illustrated could have been produced with the traditional pen, ink and nib, only a rapidograph could achieve the smooth, consistent line work as seen in the seat of the chair.

The subject was modelled by the use of hatching and crosshatching many fine lines to give the impression of depth and contour. To create deep, dark shadows, the artist put layers of strokes one over the other. Note that where line was used within the coat, it was softened and blurred by the use of crosshatching.

Materials

Surface
Cartridge paper

Size
11in × 14.5in (27cm × 36cm)

Tools
Rapidograph
Medium nib pen
HB pencil

Colors
Black rapidograph ink

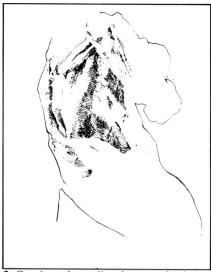

1. With an HB pencil, lightly sketch in the subject. Use a rapidograph and black ink to develop shadow tones with hatching and crosshatching.

3. With a light line, put in the shape of the chair seat. With light, loose strokes, hatch in tone of the chair seat, crosshatching to create the shadow area.

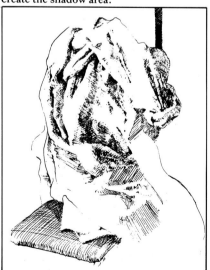

5. Put in the background shadow with broad, diagonal lines, crosshatching lightly to create darker tones.

2. Continue the outline downward using a light touch. Work into the line with hatching to create an impression of shadows and folds.

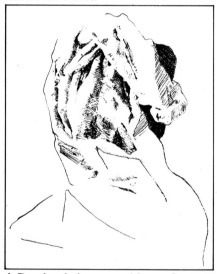

4. Develop darker areas with very fine hatching strokes. Strengthen dark outlines within the shadow areas.

6. Continue to create background shadow area by crosshatching. Vary the direction of the line within these areas.

Creating tone

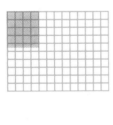

With a fine-nibbed pen, the artist blocks in light strokes of ink. These can either be left as they are to create a soft grey tone or worked over with diagonal crosshatching to create a denser shadow area.